OFFICIAL SQA PAST PAPERS WITH ANSWERS

INTERMEDIATE 2

ENGLISH
2009-2013

HODDER GIBSON
LEARN MORE

SQA

Hodder Gibson is grateful to the copyright holders, as credited on the final page of the Question Section, for permission to use their material. Every effort has been made to trace the copyright holders and to obtain their permission for the use of copyright material. Hodder Gibson will be happy to receive information allowing us to rectify any error or omission in future editions.

Hachette UK's policy is to use papers that are natural, renewable and recyclable products and made from wood grown in sustainable forests. The logging and manufacturing processes are expected to conform to the environmental regulations of the country of origin.

Orders: please contact Bookpoint Ltd, 130 Park Drive, Abingdon, Oxon OX14 4SE. Telephone: (44) 01235 827720. Fax: (44) 01235 400454.

Lines are open 9.00–5.00, Monday to Saturday, with a 24-hour message answering service. Visit our website at www.hoddereducation.co.uk. Hodder Gibson can be contacted direct on: Tel: 0141 848 1609; Fax: 0141 889 6315; email: hoddergibson@hodder.co.uk

This collection first published in 2013 by

Hodder Gibson, an imprint of Hodder Education,

An Hachette UK Company

2a Christie Street

Paisley PA1 1NB

{BrightRED   Hodder Gibson is grateful to Bright Red Publishing Ltd for collaborative work in preparation of this book and all SQA Past Paper and National 5 Model Paper titles 2013.

Typeset by PDQ Digital Media Solutions Ltd, Bungay, Suffolk NR35 1BY

Printed in the UK

A catalogue record for this title is available from the British Library

ISBN 978-1-4718-0249-2

3 2 1

2014 2013

Introduction

Study Skills – what you need to know to pass exams!

Pause for thought

Many students might skip quickly through a page like this. After all, we all know how to revise. Do you really though?

Think about this:

"IF YOU ALWAYS DO WHAT YOU ALWAYS DO, YOU WILL ALWAYS GET WHAT YOU HAVE ALWAYS GOT."

Do you like the grades you get? Do you want to do better? If you get full marks in your assessment, then that's great! Change nothing! This section is just to help you get that little bit better than you already are.

There are two main parts to the advice on offer here. The first part highlights fairly obvious things but which are also very important. The second part makes suggestions about revision that you might not have thought about but which WILL help you.

Part 1

DOH! It's so obvious but …

Start revising in good time

Don't leave it until the last minute – this will make you panic.

Make a revision timetable that sets out work time AND play time.

Sleep and eat!

Obvious really, and very helpful. Avoid arguments or stressful things too – even games that wind you up. You need to be fit, awake and focused!

Know your place!

Make sure you know exactly **WHEN and WHERE** your exams are.

Know your enemy!

Make sure you know what to expect in the exam.

How is the paper structured?

How much time is there for each question?

What types of question are involved?

Which topics seem to come up time and time again?

Which topics are your strongest and which are your weakest?

Are all topics compulsory or are there choices?

Learn by DOING!

There is no substitute for past papers and practice papers – they are simply essential! Tackling this collection of papers and answers is exactly the right thing to be doing as your exams approach.

Part 2

People learn in different ways. Some like low light, some bright. Some like early morning, some like evening / night. Some prefer warm, some prefer cold. But everyone uses their BRAIN and the brain works when it is active. Passive learning – sitting gazing at notes – is the most INEFFICIENT way to learn anything. Below you will find tips and ideas for making your revision more effective and maybe even more enjoyable. What follows gets your brain active, and active learning works!

Activity 1 – Stop and review

Step 1

When you have done no more than 5 minutes of revision reading STOP!

Step 2

Write a heading in your own words which sums up the topic you have been revising.

Step 3

Write a summary of what you have revised in no more than two sentences. Don't fool yourself by saying, 'I know it but I cannot put it into words'. That just means you don't know it well enough. If you cannot write your summary, revise that section again, knowing that you must write a summary at the end of it. Many of you will have notebooks full of blue/black ink writing. Many of the pages will not be especially attractive or memorable so try to liven them up a bit with colour as you are reviewing and rewriting. **This is a great memory aid, and memory is the most important thing.**

Activity 2 — Use technology!

Why should everything be written down? Have you thought about 'mental' maps, diagrams, cartoons and colour to help you learn? And rather than write down notes, why not record your revision material?

What about having a text message revision session with friends? Keep in touch with them to find out how and what they are revising and share ideas and questions.

Why not make a video diary where you tell the camera what you are doing, what you think you have learned and what you still have to do? No one has to see or hear it but the process of having to organise your thoughts in a formal way to explain something is a very important learning practice.

Be sure to make use of electronic files. You could begin to summarise your class notes. Your typing might be slow but it will get faster and the typed notes will be easier to read than the scribbles in your class notes. Try to add different fonts and colours to make your work stand out. You can easily Google relevant pictures, cartoons and diagrams which you can copy and paste to make your work more attractive and **MEMORABLE**.

Activity 3 – This is it. Do this and you will know lots!

Step 1

In this task you must be very honest with yourself! Find the SQA syllabus for your subject (www.sqa.org.uk). Look at how it is broken down into main topics called MANDATORY knowledge. That means stuff you MUST know.

Step 2

BEFORE you do ANY revision on this topic, write a list of everything that you already know about the subject. It might be quite a long list but you only need to write it once. It shows you all the information that is already in your long-term memory so you know what parts you do not need to revise!

Step 3

Pick a chapter or section from your book or revision notes. Choose a fairly large section or a whole chapter to get the most out of this activity.

With a buddy, use Skype, Facetime, Twitter or any other communication you have, to play the game "If this is the answer, what is the question?". For example, if you are revising Geography and the answer you provide is "meander", your buddy would have to make up a question like "What is the word that describes a feature of a river where it flows slowly and bends often from side to side?".

Make up 10 "answers" based on the content of the chapter or section you are using. Give this to your buddy to solve while you solve theirs.

Step 4

Construct a wordsearch of at least 10 X 10 squares. You can make it as big as you like but keep it realistic. Work together with a group of friends. Many apps allow you to make wordsearch puzzles online. The words and phrases can go in any direction and phrases can be split. Your puzzle must only contain facts linked to the topic you are revising. Your task is to find 10 bits of information to hide in your puzzle but you must not repeat information that you used in Step 3. DO NOT show where the words are. Fill up empty squares with random letters. Remember to keep a note of where your answers are hidden but do not show your friends. When you have a complete puzzle, exchange it with a friend to solve each other's puzzle.

Step 5

Now make up 10 questions (not "answers" this time) based on the same chapter used in the previous two tasks. Again, you must find NEW information that you have not yet used. Now it's getting hard to find that new information! Again, give your questions to a friend to answer.

Step 6

As you have been doing the puzzles, your brain has been actively searching for new information. Now write a NEW LIST that contains only the new information you have discovered when doing the puzzles. Your new list is the one to look at repeatedly for short bursts over the next few days. Try to remember more and more of it without looking at it. After a few days, you should be able to add words from your second list to your first list as you increase the information in your long-term memory.

FINALLY! Be inspired...

Make a list of different revision ideas and beside each one write **THINGS I HAVE** tried, **THINGS I WILL** try and **THINGS I MIGHT** try. Don't be scared of trying something new.

And remember – "FAIL TO PREPARE AND PREPARE TO FAIL!"

Intermediate 2 English

The course

Intermediate 2 English will give you the opportunity to develop your skills in English, literacy and communication. It is a worthwhile qualification in itself (and can help you to get into college or employment), but it is also an excellent preparation for Higher English. You will read, discuss, and write about interesting texts throughout the course, and be given an opportunity to express yourself in your Folio of Writing.

How the course is graded

Your grade in Intermediate 2 English depends on two things:

- your Folio of Writing — this is submitted to the SQA for marking and counts for 20% of your final grade
- the two exam papers you sit in May.

The exams

The Close Reading paper is one hour long and there are 30 marks available. In this paper you have to read a passage of non-fiction writing (about 1,000 words long), and answer questions on it. You will be tested on your skills of understanding, analysis and evaluation.

The Critical Essay paper is 1 hour 30 minutes long and there are 50 marks available. In this paper you have to write two essays about the texts you have studied during your course.

The SQA gives detailed advice in the Candidate Guidance Information section of the Intermediate 2 English page on its website.

Close Reading

Try to read as much as you can. Try to read some non-fiction such as articles from newspapers. This is the kind of writing you should expect to see in the Close Reading section of the exam. Most people find the passages interesting and can read and understand them, so don't be too worried about not understanding the Close Reading passage in the exam. It won't be too long either — about 1000 words. There will be the occasional word that you are not sure about, but you should be able to work out what most words mean from the clues in other words around them.

Try to give yourself the best possible chance by answering all the questions. Most people manage to do this. The questions will take you through the passage in order. Read them carefully and follow the instructions given. Be careful to look in the correct places for your answers: in nearly all questions you will be shown where

to look in the passage by line number references. It is a good idea to draw a line across your exam paper at the beginning and the end of the section you have been directed to. (Or you could use a highlighter).

'In your own words questions'

Watch out for questions which ask you to use your own words. Many people lose marks here. "**In your own words**" will be printed in bold wherever it is needed. Sometimes this type of question will ask to find a small number of words (called an "expression") from the passage, and then put them into your own words. This is almost like a translation: try to substitute words that mean roughly the same into the expression you have chosen. Don't worry if you think there are words which are impossible to change. It is not always possible to find alternative words. Another type of "own words" question is a kind of summary: you might be asked to find the writer's main points/ideas from a particular section. Here, look at the number of marks available, and try to find the same number of points.

Questions about techniques

For questions about the techniques used by the writer (analysis questions), aim to give as full an explanation of the technique, and how it adds to the writer's meaning, as you can. Most people can find a simile, or a metaphor, etc. (and are given credit for doing so), but lose marks because they can't explain the effects. They can point to examples of techniques, but are less successful in providing an explanation. Try to practise this.

Questions about word choice

In questions about the writer's word choice, pick out a word or an expression from the passage and make a comment on the actual word(s) you have chosen. Don't make a general comment about the writer's use of words (e.g. "the word choice is very negative").

Try to have an awareness of how the writer has put his or her piece of writing together — the structure. If you are asked about how a sentence helps to link ideas, look for words that point forward, or back, and quote them. You might be asked about the ending of the piece. Look for words/ideas from the ending which repeat or sum up earlier ideas.

Critical Essay

Most people sitting the exam find no real difficulty in selecting two questions from the Critical Essay paper. The questions are designed to give you the opportunity to show what you have learned about the texts you have studied. You will have to prepare/revise the texts you have studied, but try not to worry about things "not coming up."

The questions usually ask you to do two things. Make sure that you do both. One of the common mistakes is to concentrate on just one aspect of the question. This would seriously damage your mark. The most important thing is to try to answer the question. Even though you won't have a lot of time, try to make a quick plan before you write each essay. Once you have decided on a question, try to note down six or seven things that you want to say in answer to it. Jot them down on your question paper. This could make up a simple plan for your essay. Make sure you address the key words of the question in the first paragraph of your essay, and go back to these key words throughout.

As you prepare for the exam try to have a clear idea in your head what the texts you are planning to answer on are about — the themes and ideas. If you are clear in your mind about these things you will be able to answer the questions more successfully. If you don't have a good grasp of the main ideas/themes, and you don't write about them, your essay will end up looking like a list of notes.

Many people worry about learning quotes from the texts they have studied, and think that they have to fit every quote they have learned into their essays. For drama and poetry you will certainly be expected to include some quotes, but only ones that would be relevant to the question you are answering. Don't be concerned if you don't get the opportunity to use all of your quotes. When writing about a novel, quotes are much less important. When dealing with a novel or short story it is much more important to write about key episodes, and to describe the main characters and setting, etc.

Keep an eye on the accuracy of your writing in the exam. Remember to divide your writing into paragraphs, and make sure you write in sentences (full stops and capital letters).

The main thing to remember is — answer the question.

Good luck!

Remember that the rewards for passing Intermediate 2 English are well worth it! Your pass will help you get the future you want for yourself. In the exam, be confident in your own ability. If you're not sure how to answer a question trust your own instincts and give it a go anyway - keep calm and don't panic! GOOD LUCK!

INTERMEDIATE 2

2009

[BLANK PAGE]

X115/201

NATIONAL
QUALIFICATIONS
2009

FRIDAY, 15 MAY
1.00 PM – 2.00 PM

ENGLISH
INTERMEDIATE 2
Close Reading

Answer all questions.

30 marks are allocated to this paper.

Read the passage carefully and then answer **all** the questions, **using your own words as far as possible**.

The questions will ask you to show that:

> you understand the main ideas and important details in the passage—in other words, **what** the writer has said (**Understanding–U**);

> you can identify, using appropriate terms, the techniques the writer has used to get across these ideas—in other words, **how** he has said it (**Analysis–A**);

> you can, using appropriate evidence, comment on how effective the writer has been—in other words, **how well** he has said it (**Evaluation–E**).

A code letter (U, A, E) is used alongside each question to identify its purpose for you. The number of marks attached to each question will give some indication of the length of answer required.

Why Dickens was the hero of Soweto

In this passage, the writer informs us about the effect that books by Charles Dickens, a 19th-century English writer, had on black South African children during the time of racial segregation ("apartheid") in South Africa. "Afrikaans" was the form of Dutch spoken in South Africa by some white rulers before the arrival of democracy in that country.

Hector Pieterson was 12 when he died.   Today a museum bearing his name commemorates his death—and hundreds of others—which occurred some 30 years ago at a place whose name has come to symbolise uprising against oppression: Soweto.

Hector was one of thousands of black children who took to the streets on June 16, 1976,
5 in protest about schooling under the apartheid regime in South Africa.   When police opened fire on the march it brought the word Soweto to the attention of the world.   But less well known is the role that Charles Dickens played in events.

The march was in protest at a government edict making Afrikaans compulsory in schools.   From January 1976, half of all subjects were to be taught in it, including ones in
10 which difficulties of translation were often an issue.

To pupils accustomed to being educated in English, the Afrikaans policy was the last of a line of insults delivered in the name of "Bantu" or "native education".   They thought being taught in Afrikaans, the language of a regime that had tried to "unpeople" them, would cost them their last remaining freedom—that of thinking for themselves, using
15 their minds.

That is where Dickens came in.   Many books were banned under apartheid but not the classics of English literature.   Pupils arriving hungry at school every day were captivated by the story of a frail but courageous boy named Oliver Twist.

The book was a revelation.   Systemised oppression of children happened in England too!
20 They were not alone.   Slave labour, thin rations and cruel taunts were part of a child's life in the world outside as well.

One former pupil, now in his forties, says of Dickens: "Four or five of us would be together and discuss the stories.   And to think he wasn't banned!   The authorities didn't know what was in these books, how they helped us to be strong, to think that we were
25 not forgotten."

Not being forgotten was particularly crucial.   The apartheid regime had tried to "vanish" black people.   Feeling abandoned and isolated, people turned to Dickens as someone who understood their plight.

But there were not enough books to go round.   Few of the crateloads of Shakespeare,
30 Hardy and Dickens shipped from Britain reached the townships.   Instead, they came to Soweto in parcels from charities.   They were read by candlelight, often out loud, shared in a circle, or passed from hand to hand.

At Morris Isaacson School, one of the moving forces behind the Soweto protest, which produced two of its leaders, Murphy Morobe, "Shakespeare's best friend in Africa", and
35 Tsietsi Mashinini, there were 1,500 pupils and three copies of *Oliver Twist* in 1976. The former pupils recall waiting months for their turn, with a similar wait for *Nicholas Nickleby*.

But it was Oliver that they took to heart: students at one of the country's leading black colleges, Lovedale, formed a committee to ask for more.

40 Calling it the Board, after Dickens's Board of Guardians, they asked for more lessons, more food—and more and better books. Their reward was to be charged with public violence. All 152 "board" members were expelled from the college and some were jailed.

They felt that Dickens was obviously on their side. Descriptions of Gamfield's "ugly leer" and Bumble's "repulsive countenance" and Oliver being beaten by Mrs

45 Sowerberry and shoved "but nothing daunted" into the dust-cellar were evidence that this English author understood the plight of black South Africans.

Dickens's compassion for the poor linked the people of Soweto to a worldwide literature of tremendous importance.

The veteran South African trumpeter Hugh Masekela later chose *Nicholas Nickleby* as

50 his favourite book on a popular radio programme, *Desert Island Discs*, telling the presenter what its author did for people in the townships: "He taught us suffering is the same everywhere."

The love of books that enabled an author dead for more than 100 years to inspire thousands of schoolchildren came mainly from grandmothers who had educated their

55 families orally, then urged them to read widely and learn all that they could.

It also came from people such as the activist Steve Biko, whose own mentor, the Brazilian educator Paulo Freire, spent a lifetime working with forest people who had no formal education, teaching them to "name the world their own way".

That is what the youth of Soweto wanted—a future in their own words. And they got it.

60 "Africans are not dustbins," declared some of the June 16 placards; and "Beware of Afrikaans, the most dangerous drug for our future." By the following year, the language had been withdrawn from classrooms as unworkable. And so, thanks to the influence of a long-dead British author, the sacrifices of Hector Pieterson and many other Africans have proved to be not entirely in vain —which Dickens himself would surely applaud.

Adapted from an article by Carol Lee in *The Times*, 10th June, 2006

QUESTIONS

Marks Code

1. Explain fully any way in which the writer makes the opening paragraph dramatic.

2 A

2. The writer tells us that Soweto "has come to symbolise uprising against oppression" (line 3).

   Write down one expression from the next paragraph (lines 4–7) which continues the idea of uprising, **and** one which continues the idea of oppression.

2 U

3. Explain **in your own words**

   (a) what the marchers were objecting to, according to lines 8–10;

2 U

   (b) why this issue was so important to them, according to lines 11–15.

1 U

4. Look at lines 16–25.

   (a) Explain **in your own words** why Dickens's books were not "banned under apartheid" (line 16).

1 U

   (b) **In your own words** explain why Dickens's book *Oliver Twist* would have "captivated" the Soweto children.

2 U

5. Explain the purpose of the exclamation mark in line 23.

1 A

6. "But there were not enough books to go round." (line 29)

   (a) Explain how this sentence provides a link between paragraphs at this point.

2 A

   (b) Explain fully how the paragraph between lines 33 and 37 illustrates the idea that there were not enough books to go round.

2 A

7. Explain why the writer's use of "reward" in line 41 is ironic.

2 A

8. Explain why the writer's use of examples from the writing of Dickens in lines 43 to 46 is effective in advancing her argument at this point.

3 E

9. Look at lines 49–52.

   Explain **in your own words** why Hugh Masekela thought Dickens was so important.

2 U

10. Explain **in your own words** how the grandmothers referred to in line 54 instilled a love of books in their grandchildren.

2 U

11. Explain how any aspect of the **structure** of the paragraph in line 59 contributes to its effectiveness.

2 A

12. Look at the placard text "Beware of Afrikaans, the most dangerous drug for our future". (lines 60–61)

    Explain why this expression is an effective image or metaphor.

2 A/E

13. Look at the last paragraph of the passage (lines 60–64).

    Explain fully why this provides an effective conclusion to the passage.

2 A/E

Total (30)

[END OF QUESTION PAPER]

X115/202

NATIONAL
QUALIFICATIONS
2009

FRIDAY, 15 MAY
2.20 PM – 3.50 PM

ENGLISH
INTERMEDIATE 2
Critical Essay

Answer **two** questions.

Each question must be taken from a different section.

Each question is worth 25 marks.

SQA

Answer TWO questions from this paper.

Each question must be chosen from a different Section (A–E). You are not allowed to choose two questions from the same Section.

In all Sections you may use Scottish texts.

Write the number of each question in the margin of your answer booklet and begin each essay on a fresh page.

You should spend about 45 minutes on each essay.

The following will be assessed:

- **the relevance of your essays to the questions you have chosen**
- **your knowledge and understanding of key elements, central concerns and significant details of the chosen texts**
- **your explanation of ways in which aspects of structure/style/language contribute to the meaning/effect/impact of the chosen texts**
- **your evaluation of the effectiveness of the chosen texts, supported by detailed and relevant evidence**
- **the quality and technical accuracy of your writing.**

Each question is worth 25 marks. The total for this paper is 50 marks.

SECTION A—DRAMA

Answers to questions in this section should refer to the text and to such relevant features as: characterisation, key scene(s), structure, climax, theme, plot, conflict, setting . . .

1. Choose a character from a play whose fate is unfortunate or unhappy.

   Show how much of the character's misfortune is caused by the personality and decisions of the character and how much by other circumstances in the play.

2. Choose a scene from a play in which suspense or tension is built up.

   Show how this suspense or tension is built up and what effect this scene has on the play as a whole.

3. Choose a play which deals with a close relationship within a family or a community.

   Show how the portrayal of the relationship helps in your understanding of the central concerns of the play.

SECTION B—PROSE

Answers to questions in this section should refer to the text and to such relevant features as: characterisation, setting, language, key incident(s), climax/turning point, plot, structure, narrative technique, theme, ideas, description . . .

4. Choose a novel **or** a short story in which a character is in conflict with his or her friends or relatives or society.

   Show how the conflict arises and what effect it has on the character's fate in the novel or short story as a whole.

5. Choose a novel **or** a short story which deals with the effects of evil or war or deceit or a breakdown in society or a breakdown in relationship(s).

   Show how any of these negative pressures affects the main character in the novel or short story and go on to show whether or not she or he tackles it successfully.

6. Choose a **non-fiction** text **or** group of texts which interests you because of its detailed and vivid description of scenes, events, people.

   Show how the detailed description makes the scenes, events, people vivid for you and increases your understanding of what is happening.

SECTION C—POETRY

Answers to questions in this section should refer to the text and to such relevant features as: word choice, tone, imagery, structure, content, rhythm, theme, sound, ideas . . .

7. Choose a poem which deals with childhood, adolescence, family life or old age.

   Show how the poet deepens your understanding of any of these stages of life by the choice of content and the skilful use of poetic techniques.

8. Choose a poem which deals with a particular time of year or a particular place.

   Show how the poet, by his or her choice of content and style, persuades you to adopt his or her view of the season or the place.

9. Choose a poem which has as one of its central concerns a personal, social or religious issue.

   Show how the content and the poetic techniques used increase your understanding of the issue.

[Turn over

SECTION D—FILM AND TV DRAMA

Answers to questions in this section should refer to the text and to such relevant features as: use of camera, key sequence, characterisation, mise-en-scène, editing, setting, music/sound effects, plot, dialogue . . .

10. Choose a film **or** TV drama* which both entertains and helps to raise awareness of social issues.

    Show how the film or TV drama you have chosen succeeds in both these aspects.

11. Choose a sequence from a film which is important both to the atmosphere and to the plot of the film.

    Show how atmosphere is created in the sequence and go on to show how the sequence and the atmosphere are important to the film as a whole.

12. Choose a film **or** TV drama* which is set **either** in a past age **or** in the future.

    Show how the director/programme-maker has created the setting of the past **or** the future and go on to show how the setting increases your enjoyment of the film or TV drama.

    * "TV drama" includes a single play, a series or a serial.

SECTION E—LANGUAGE

Answers to questions in this section should refer to the text and to such relevant features as: register, accent, dialect, slang, jargon, vocabulary, tone, abbreviation . . .

13. Consider how TV programmes aimed at young audiences have an effect on the language young people use.

    Identify any recent changes in vocabulary or accent that you are aware of and explain whether you feel the new words/accents are more effective in communicating than those which they have replaced.

14. Consider the use of emotive language in any form of advertising with which you are familiar.

    By referring to specific examples show how effective you feel the use of emotive language is in its particular context.

15. Consider the distinctive language found in any group of people with a shared interest in a sport, hobby, job or activity.

    By referring to specific examples of distinctive vocabulary or codes or grammatical forms show whether or not these features increase the effectiveness of communication within the group.

[END OF QUESTION PAPER]

INTERMEDIATE 2

2010

[BLANK PAGE]

X115/201

NATIONAL
QUALIFICATIONS
2010

THURSDAY, 13 MAY
1.00 PM – 2.00 PM

ENGLISH
INTERMEDIATE 2
Close Reading

Answer all questions.

30 marks are allocated to this paper.

Read the passage carefully and then answer **all** the questions, **using your own words as far as possible**.

The questions will ask you to show that:

> you understand the main ideas and important details in the passage—in other words, **what** the writer has said (**Understanding—U**);

> you can identify, using appropriate terms, the techniques the writer has used to get across these ideas—in other words, **how** he has said it (**Analysis—A**);

> you can, using appropriate evidence, comment on how effective the writer has been—in other words, **how well** he has said it (**Evaluation—E**).

A code letter (U, A, E) is used alongside each question to identify its purpose for you. The number of marks attached to each question will give some indication of the length of answer required.

The Mighty Qin

This piece was written round about the time that an exhibition of some of the warriors from the ancient Chinese Terracotta Army was on display in the British Museum in London.

Qin Shi Who? My reaction entirely. I had heard of the Terracotta Army, of course. I had even seen some of them when a vanguard of warriors came to London in the 1980s. But I couldn't have told you who Qin Shihuangdi (pronounced *Chin Shur Hwang Dee*) was. Even if you'd said he was the First Emperor of China, I'd have had only the haziest
5 recollection of what you were talking about.

That probably goes for the vast majority of people in the West. And given that he is one of the most colossal figures ever to have walked the earth, that is rather shocking. For Qin Shihuangdi, its First Emperor, created China more than two millennia ago, establishing the world's longest-lasting empire. A visionary, a brutal tyrant and a
10 megalomaniac, he is the greatest historical figure that most of us have never heard of.

I only began to grasp this a few months ago when I travelled to Xi'an to visit the First Emperor's mind-boggling mausoleum, home to his Terracotta Army. "This is one of the people who changed the world," said Neil MacGregor, director of the British Museum. "There are terribly few historical figures whose achievements lasted like that.
15 This is really one of the great, great figures in human history."

The written historical sources for the man who bequeathed his name to his country are scant. Born Ying Zheng in 259 BC, he was the son of the king of Qin, in central China. He succeeded at the age of 13 and there was a period when he ruled with a regent. Then, when he was properly established on the throne, he embarked on what was
20 China's only real revolution until the 20th century.

Through clever diplomacy and brilliant military strategy he conquered and subdued neighbouring states. He achieved this by developing a highly organised army. Qin chariots had an improved design of smaller wheels with more spokes that provided greater stability and durability. The width of axles was made uniform, a seemingly small
25 innovation with massive repercussions: the chariots could ride relatively smoothly down the same ruts in the road and so avoid churning up the entire highway. The light infantry were armed with extremely sharp bronze weapons and crossbows and supported by cavalry.

This formidable war machine brought the warring states under the control of Qin, and
30 the heart of the area that we now call China was united for the first time in 221 BC. Ying Zheng decided to mark the success by renaming himself Qin Shihuangdi, or First Emperor of Qin.

The first Emperor survived at least three assassination attempts in subsequent years, incidents that served to tighten his grip on every aspect of life. He created a surveillance
35 culture in which neighbours were expected to spy on each other and lived in fear of terrible punishments for failing to do so or for breaking the many laws. One of the most miserable punishments, which very often proved to be a death sentence, was to be dispatched into the wilderness to toil on the construction of the wall Qin Shihuangdi had ordered to be built along the northern frontier of the empire.

40 Although there had been a tradition of building walls to mark the boundaries of territory and keep neighbours out, the First Emperor's undertaking was the most significant building project to date, aiming to protect the borders from nomads. His wall was rather farther north than what we think of today as the Great Wall, which is the series of fortifications (not one single wall) built in the Ming Dynasty, which ruled China for

45 almost three centuries from 1368. Little of the Qin wall remains beyond a few mounds that are believed to be from the First Emperor's era. But he is regarded as the grandfather of the Great Wall, that iconic symbol of China's historical separateness and age-old industriousness.

The First Emperor's imprint on the lives of the inhabitants of his far-flung kingdoms
50 was seen further. He unified the script, demanding that all states write the pictographs of ancient Chinese in the same way. So, although the words might be pronounced differently in different parts of the empire, once they were written down everyone who could read could understand each other, a particular advantage for traders. Some of the pictographs are recognisable in the language today, and the principle of a single written
55 language that can be spoken in different ways remains.

But for the First Emperor, establishing complete control over his empire was not enough. He wanted to rule forever. If he couldn't have immortality in this world, the next best thing would be to rule in the nether world. We knew about his tomb mound because the ancient sources referred to it, and it has always been there.

60 The tomb itself may never be opened because of the sensitivities of disturbing the Emperor, although some archaeologists hope that improved technology may one day allow some form of exploration.

The ancient sources refer to 700,000 people labouring on the tomb, but make no reference to what else the Emperor had devised under the ground. This is presumably
65 because they didn't know about his subterranean empire, which lay undisturbed until 1974. Those of the 600 pits that have been examined have yielded almost 1,800 mass-produced clay figures with another 6,000 believed to exist. In this mountain fastness Qin Shihuangdi wanted an army to protect him from his enemies, but also wanted his civil servants on hand and musicians and acrobats to entertain him.

70 "I can't think of anyone else who had the scale of ambition to think of replicating their entire kingdom," says MacGregor. "Nobody else in human history has attempted to do that, and what is fascinating is that it's the eternal underground that has survived and nothing else. We have no buildings, we have no writings, this is all that survives. The people making the figures knew they were making them to serve the Emperor and live
75 forever. And in a funny way they have."

The Emperor went to his tomb rather earlier than he had intended. In 210 BC, on one of his imperial progresses, he fell ill and died in his carriage.

There is no substitute for seeing the mass ranks of the Terracotta Army. But the British Museum wants to do two things: show visitors a selection of warriors up close in a way
80 that is not possible in Xi'an, and tell the story of the man whose breathtaking megalomania gave us one of the wonders of the world. The telling of that story is long overdue.

Damian Whitworth in *The Times*

QUESTIONS

Marks Code

1. Looking in the opening paragraph (lines 1–5) for your answer, explain **in your own words** what the writer's original "reaction" to the name Qin Shihuangdi was.

    1 U

2. The first paragraph (lines 1–5) is written in a chatty style. Identify **one** expression or feature from these lines which contributes to this chattiness, and explain why it does so.

    2 A

3. Look at paragraph 2 (lines 6–10).

    Give **in your own words two** reasons why it is "rather shocking" that most people in the West do not know about Qin.

    2 U

4. Show how any **one** feature of Neil MacGregor's word choice (see lines 12–15) makes it clear that he thinks of Qin as someone special.

    2 A

5. Explain **in your own words two** of the consequences of the improvements Qin made to his war chariots (see lines 24–26).

    2 U

6. How appropriate is the expression "formidable war machine" (line 29) at this point in the passage?

    3 E

7. Explain **in your own words** any **two** ways in which Qin managed to "tighten his grip on every aspect of life" (line 34).

    2 U

8. What does the writer gain by using "toil" (line 38) rather than the word "work"?

    1 A

9. The writer calls the Great Wall an "iconic symbol" (line 47).

    (*a*) Why is it appropriate to call the wall a "symbol"?

    1 A/E

    (*b*) **In your own words**, explain fully what aspects of China it symbolises.

    3 U

10. Explain how the sentence "But for the First Emperor, establishing complete control over his empire was not enough." (lines 56–57) works as a link between paragraphs at this point.

    2 A

11. Show fully how the writer introduces a **tone** of doubt when he writes about the prospects for opening the tomb (lines 60–62).

    2 A

12. How does the writer convey the grandness or large scale of the tomb in lines 63–69? You should refer to technique as well as content.

    2 A

13. Show how an aspect of what Neil MacGregor says (lines 70–75) effectively conveys his sense of wonder.

    Your answer should refer to an example of **word choice or structure**.

    2 E

14. In what sense does the writer use "funny" in line 75?

    1 U

15. Explain why any example of the **word choice** in the final paragraph (lines 78–82) contributes to a neat conclusion to the passage.

    2 A

Total (30)

[END OF QUESTION PAPER]

X115/202

NATIONAL QUALIFICATIONS 2010	THURSDAY, 13 MAY 2.20 PM – 3.50 PM	ENGLISH INTERMEDIATE 2 Critical Essay

Answer **two** questions.

Each question must be taken from a different section.

Each question is worth 25 marks.

Answer TWO questions from this paper.

Each question must be chosen from a different Section (A–E). You are not allowed to choose two questions from the same Section.

In all Sections you may use Scottish texts.

Write the number of each question in the margin of your answer booklet and begin each essay on a fresh page.

You should spend about 45 minutes on each essay.

The following will be assessed:

- **the relevance of your essays to the questions you have chosen**

- **your knowledge and understanding of key elements, central concerns and significant details of the chosen texts**

- **your explanation of ways in which aspects of structure/style/language contribute to the meaning/effect/impact of the chosen texts**

- **your evaluation of the effectiveness of the chosen texts, supported by detailed and relevant evidence**

- **the quality and technical accuracy of your writing.**

Each question is worth 25 marks. The total for this paper is 50 marks.

SECTION A—DRAMA

Answers to questions in this section should refer to the text and to such relevant features as: characterisation, key scene(s), structure, climax, theme, plot, conflict, setting . . .

1. Choose a play in which a central character feels increasingly isolated from those around her or him.

   Explain why the character finds herself or himself isolated, and show what the consequences are for the character concerned.

2. Choose a scene from a play in which there is an important incident which leads to a turning point in the action.

   Explain what happens in the scene, and then go on to say how it affects the outcome of the play.

3. Choose a play in which one of the main concerns is love **or** jealousy **or** betrayal **or** reconciliation.

   Explain what the concern is, and show how it is explored throughout the play.

SECTION B—PROSE

Answers to questions in this section should refer to the text and to such relevant features as: characterisation, setting, language, key incident(s), climax, turning point, plot, structure, narrative technique, theme, ideas, description . . .

4. Choose a novel **or** a short story which gives you an insight into an aspect of human nature or behaviour.

   State what the aspect is, and show how the characters' actions and relationships lead you to a deeper understanding of human nature or behaviour.

5. Choose a novel **or** a short story with an ending which you find satisfactory.

   By looking at the novel or short story as a whole, explain why you find the ending satisfactory in bringing to a conclusion the main concerns of the text.

6. Choose a prose work (fiction **or** non-fiction) in which setting is an important feature.

   Explain how the writer creates the setting, and then go on to show how this feature contributes to your understanding of the text as a whole.

SECTION C—POETRY

Answers to questions in this section should refer to the text and to such relevant features as: word choice, tone, imagery, structure, content, rhythm, theme, sound, ideas . . .

7. Choose a poem which could be considered as having a powerful message.

   Show how the poet effectively conveys this message through his or her use of poetic techniques.

8. Choose a poem in which the poet creates a particular mood or atmosphere.

   Show how the poet creates this mood or atmosphere by his or her choice of subject matter and use of poetic techniques.

9. Choose a poem which portrays an interesting character.

   Show how the poet uses poetic techniques to make the character interesting.

[Turn over

SECTION D—FILM AND TV DRAMA

> *Answers to questions in this section should refer to the text and to such relevant features as: use of camera, key sequence, characterisation, mise-en-scène, editing, setting, music/sound, special effects, plot, dialogue . . .*

10. Choose a film **or** TV drama* which deals with issues which mainly affect young people.

    Explain how the film or TV drama* deals with such issues, stating whether or not you find the portrayal of these issues realistic.

11. Choose a scene or sequence from a film or TV drama* which provides a climax to the action.

    Briefly describe the events leading up to the climax, and then explain how the techniques used by the film or programme makers create a heightened sense of importance in this scene or sequence.

12. Choose a film which you think is typical of its genre, for example: action, romance, comedy, horror . . .

    Explain how the film makers have used the features of the genre to create a successful film.

  * "TV drama" includes a single play, a series or a serial.

SECTION E—LANGUAGE

> *Answers to questions in this section should refer to the text and to such relevant features as: register, accent, dialect, slang, jargon, vocabulary, tone, abbreviation . . .*

13. Consider a text which you find to be persuasive, for example: an advertisement, a speech, a newspaper article . . .

    By referring to specific examples from your chosen text, show how persuasive techniques have been used to convince you.

14. Consider the ways that young people use the internet to communicate and socialise, for example: networking sites, instant messaging, chat rooms, blogs . . .

    By referring to specific examples of language and vocabulary, explain how such communication differs from formal English, and what its attractions are for young people.

15. Consider the specialist language used by any group which has a common leisure, vocational or geographical connection.

    Show how the specialist language used by the group is effective in communicating shared interests accurately.

[END OF QUESTION PAPER]

INTERMEDIATE 2

2011

[BLANK PAGE]

X270/201

NATIONAL QUALIFICATIONS 2011	FRIDAY, 13 MAY 1.00 PM – 2.00 PM	ENGLISH INTERMEDIATE 2 Close Reading

Answer all questions.

30 marks are allocated to this paper.

Read the passage carefully and then answer **all** the questions, **using your own words as far as possible**.

The questions will ask you to show that:

> you understand the main ideas and important details in the passage—in other words, **what** the writer has said (**Understanding—U**);

> you can identify, using appropriate terms, the techniques the writer has used to get across these ideas—in other words, **how** he has said it (**Analysis—A**);

> you can, using appropriate evidence, comment on how effective the writer has been—in other words, **how well** he has said it (**Evaluation—E**).

A code letter (U, A, E) is used alongside each question to identify its purpose for you. The number of marks attached to each question will give some indication of the length of answer required.

The gr8 db8

Some people say that text messaging is destroying the English language. David Crystal, an eminent professor of language, argues that it is not.

Recently, a newspaper article headed "1 h8 txt msgs: how texting is wrecking our language" argued that texters are "vandals who are doing to our language what Genghis Khan did to his neighbours 800 years ago. They are destroying it: pillaging our punctuation; savaging our sentences."

5 As a new variety of language, texting has been condemned as "textese", "slanguage", a "digital virus", "bleak, bald, sad shorthand", "drab shrinktalk which masks dyslexia, poor spelling and mental laziness".

Ever since the arrival of printing—thought to be the invention of the devil because it would put false opinions into people's minds—people have been arguing that new
10 technology would have disastrous consequences for language. Scares accompanied the introduction of the telegraph, the telephone, and broadcasting. But has there ever been a linguistic phenomenon that has aroused such curiosity, suspicion, fear, confusion, antagonism, fascination, excitement and enthusiasm all at once as texting? And in such a short space of time. Less than a decade ago, hardly anyone had heard
15 of it.

People think that the written language seen on mobile phone screens is new and alien, but all the popular beliefs about texting are wrong. Its distinctiveness is not a new phenomenon, nor is its use restricted to the young. There is increasing evidence that it helps rather than hinders literacy. Texting has added a new dimension to language
20 use, but its long-term impact is negligible. It is not a disaster.

Research has made it clear that the early media hysteria about the novelty (and thus the dangers) of text messaging was misplaced. People seem to have swallowed whole the stories that youngsters use nothing else but abbreviations when they text, such as the reports that a teenager had written an essay so full of textspeak that her teacher
25 was unable to understand it. An extract was posted online, and quoted incessantly, but, as no one was ever able to track down the entire essay, it was probably a hoax.

There are several distinctive features of the way texts are written that combine to give the impression of novelty, but people have been initialising common phrases for ages. IOU is known from 1618. There is no real difference between a modern kid's "lol"
30 ("laughing out loud") and an earlier generation's "SWALK" ("sealed with a loving kiss").

English has had abbreviated words ever since it began to be written down. Words such as exam, vet, fridge and bus are so familiar that they have effectively become new words. When some of these abbreviated forms first came into use, they also
35 attracted criticism. In 1711, for example, Joseph Addison complained about the way words were being "miserably curtailed"—he mentioned pos (itive) and incog (nito).

Texters use deviant spellings—and they know they are deviant. But they are by no means the first to use such nonstandard forms as "cos" for "because" or "wot" for "what". Several of these are so much part of English literary tradition that they have
40 been given entries in the Oxford English Dictionary. "Cos" is there from 1828 and "wot" from 1829. Many can be found in the way dialect is written by such writers as Charles Dickens, Mark Twain, Walter Scott and D.H. Lawrence.

Sending a message on a mobile phone is not the most natural of ways to communicate. The keypad isn't linguistically sensible. No one took letter-frequency
45 considerations into account when designing it. For example, key 7 on my mobile contains four symbols, pqrs. It takes four key-presses to access the letter s, and yet s is one of the most frequently occurring letters in English. It is twice as easy to input q, which is one of the least frequently occurring letters. It should be the other way round. So any strategy that reduces the time and awkwardness of inputting graphic
50 symbols is bound to be attractive.

Abbreviations were used as a natural, intuitive response to a technological problem. And they appeared in next to no time. Texters simply transferred (and then embellished) what they had encountered in other settings. We have all left notes in which we have replaced "and" with "&", "three" with "3", and so on.

55 But the need to save time and energy is by no means the whole story of texting. When we look at some texts, they are linguistically quite complex. There are an extraordinary number of ways in which people play with language—creating riddles, solving crosswords, playing Scrabble, inventing new words. Professional writers do the same—providing catchy copy for advertising slogans, thinking up puns in
60 newspaper headlines, and writing poems, novels and plays. Children quickly learn that one of the most enjoyable things you can do with language is to play with its sounds, words, grammar—and spelling.

An extraordinary number of doom-laden prophecies have been made about the supposed linguistic evils unleashed by texting. Sadly, its creative potential has been
65 virtually ignored. But children could not be good at texting if they had not already developed considerable literacy awareness. Before you can write and play with abbreviated forms, you need to have a sense of how the sounds of your language relate to the letters. You need to know that there are such things as alternative spellings. If you are aware that your texting behaviour is different, you must have already realised
70 that there is such a thing as a standard.

Some people dislike texting. Some are bemused by it. But it is merely the latest manifestation of the human ability to be linguistically creative and to adapt language to suit the demands of diverse settings. There is no disaster pending. We will not see a new generation of adults growing up unable to write proper English. The language
75 as a whole will not decline. In texting what we are seeing, in a small way, is language in evolution.

Adapted from an article
by David Crystal in *The Guardian*

QUESTIONS

Marks Code

1. Look at the opening paragraph (lines 1–4).

   (*a*) Write down **one** expression from this paragraph which continues the idea introduced by "wrecking".

   1 U

   (*b*) Identify a feature of the expression "pillaging our punctuation; savaging our sentences" which makes it effective.

   1 A

2. The writer tells us that "texting has been condemned" (line 5).

   Explain fully how any **one** of the expressions he quotes in the rest of this paragraph conveys disapproval of text message language.

   2 A

QUESTIONS (continued)   *Marks Code*

3. Why does the writer mention "the telegraph, the telephone, and broadcasting" (line 11) at this point in his argument?   2   U

4. Look at the sentence "But . . . texting?" (lines 11–13).

   (*a*) In this sentence, what point is the writer making about attitudes to texting?   1   U

   (*b*) Show how the writer's **word choice or structure** helps to reinforce this point.   1   A

5. The writer tells us (line 17) that "all the popular beliefs about texting are wrong".

   Look at the remainder of the paragraph (lines 17–20), and then explain **in your own words** what **two** of these popular beliefs are.   2   U

6. How effective do you find the writer's use of "hysteria" (line 21) as an **image** or **metaphor**?   2   E

7. The expression "swallowed whole" (line 22) suggests that people were too ready to believe what they had heard.

   Show how the writer continues this idea of gullibility in the remainder of the paragraph.   2   A

8. Why is the writer correct when he tells us that "there is no real difference" between "lol" and "SWALK" (see lines 29–31)?   1   A

9. Re-read lines 32–36, and then explain **in your own words two** points the writer is making about abbreviations.   2   U

10. Explain how effective you find the author's inclusion of the names of Dickens, Twain, Scott and Lawrence (line 42).   2   E

11. Re-read lines 43–50, and then explain **in your own words** in what ways "The keypad isn't linguistically sensible".   2   U

12. Explain why the sentence "Abbreviations were used as a natural, intuitive response to a technological problem" (line 51) is an appropriate link at this point in the passage.   2   A

13. Explain fully why the writer's use of "But" (line 55) is appropriate at this point in the structure of his argument.   3   U/A

14. What **tone** does the writer create by using the expression "supposed linguistic evils" (line 64)?   1   A

15. Look at lines 65–70, and then explain briefly **and in your own words** what the writer means when he refers to "literacy awareness" (line 66).   1   U

16. Look at the final paragraph (lines 71–76), and then explain how well you feel this paragraph works as a conclusion to the passage as a whole.   2   E

Total (30)

[*END OF QUESTION PAPER*]

X270/202

NATIONAL
QUALIFICATIONS
2011

FRIDAY, 13 MAY
2.20 PM – 3.50 PM

ENGLISH
INTERMEDIATE 2
Critical Essay

Answer **two** questions.

Each question must be taken from a different section.

Each question is worth 25 marks.

Answer TWO questions from this paper.

Each question must be chosen from a different Section (A–E). You are not allowed to choose two questions from the same Section.

In all Sections you may use Scottish texts.

Write the number of each question in the margin of your answer booklet and begin each essay on a fresh page.

You should spend about 45 minutes on each essay.

The following will be assessed:

- **the relevance of your essays to the questions you have chosen**

- **your knowledge and understanding of key elements, central concerns and significant details of the chosen texts**

- **your explanation of ways in which aspects of structure/style/language contribute to the meaning/effect/impact of the chosen texts**

- **your evaluation of the effectiveness of the chosen texts, supported by detailed and relevant evidence**

- **the quality and technical accuracy of your writing.**

Each question is worth 25 marks. The total for this paper is 50 marks.

SECTION A—DRAMA

Answers to questions in this section should refer to the text and to such relevant features as: characterisation, key scene(s), structure, climax, theme, plot, conflict, setting . . .

1. Choose a play in which there is a character who suffers from a human weakness such as ambition, selfishness, lack of self-knowledge, jealousy, pride, lust . . .

   Show how the weakness is revealed, then explain how this weakness affects both the characters and the events of the play.

2. Choose a play in which there is an important relationship between two of the main characters.

   Describe the nature of the relationship, and explain how it is developed throughout the play.

3. Choose a play which you feel has a dramatic final scene.

   Describe briefly what happens and explain how effective the ending is in bringing to a conclusion the central concerns of the text.

SECTION B—PROSE

Answers to questions in this section should refer to the text and to such relevant features as: characterisation, setting, language, key incident(s), climax, turning point, plot, structure, narrative technique, theme, ideas, description . . .

4. Choose a novel **or** a short story in which you feel there is an incident of great importance to the story as a whole.

   Describe the incident and go on to show its importance to the development of the characters and the central concerns of the text.

5. Choose a novel **or** a short story which has a character who affects you emotionally.

   Describe how you feel about the character, and show how the writer leads you to feel this way.

6. Choose a prose work (fiction **or** non-fiction) in which the writer uses a memorable style/voice/narrative technique.

   Explain in detail how features of the writing style/voice/narrative technique contribute to the effectiveness of the text.

SECTION C—POETRY

Answers to questions in this section should refer to the text and to such relevant features as: word choice, tone, imagery, structure, content, rhythm, theme, sound, ideas . . .

7. Choose a poem which deals with an important issue such as war, crime, poverty **or** racism.

   Explain how the poet deepens your understanding of the issue by the choice of content and the skilful use of poetic techniques.

8. Choose a poem which describes an animal **or** a place **or** an event in an effective way.

   Briefly state what is being described and go on to show how the techniques used in the poem make the description effective.

9. Choose a poem written in a specific form such as ballad, sonnet, elegy, monologue, ode . . .

   Explain how the distinctive features of this form contribute to your appreciation of the text.

[Turn over

SECTION D—FILM AND TV DRAMA

> *Answers to questions in this section should refer to the text and to such relevant features as: use of camera, key sequence, characterisation, mise-en-scène, editing, setting, music/sound, special effects, plot, dialogue . . .*

10. Choose a film **or** TV drama* which has a character who could be described as a hero or as a villain.

    Explain how the the character is introduced and then developed throughout the film or TV drama.

11. Choose a film **or** TV drama* in which setting is an important feature.

    Explain how the setting is established and go on to show how the setting contributes to the effectiveness of the film **or** TV drama as a whole.

12. Choose a scene or sequence from a film **or** TV drama* in which an atmosphere of mystery, **or** horror, **or** suspense is created.

    Describe what happens in the scene or sequence, explaining how the techniques used by the film or programme makers create this atmosphere.

   * "TV drama" includes a single play, a series or a serial.

SECTION E—LANGUAGE

> *Answers to questions in this section should refer to the text and to such relevant features as: register, accent, dialect, slang, jargon, vocabulary, tone, abbreviation . . .*

13. Consider a text which aims to persuade people to support a particular group, **or** to buy a particular product.

    By referring to specific examples from your chosen text, show how persuasive techniques are used.

14. Consider a modern form of communication such as e-mail **or** text message.

    By referring to specific examples of language and vocabulary, explain how such communication differs from formal English, and what advantages this presents to users.

15. Consider the specialist language used by any group of people to talk about a particular interest, for example, a sport, a job, a hobby . . .

    By referring to specific examples, show how the specialist language used by the group is effective in communicating ideas clearly.

[END OF QUESTION PAPER]

[BLANK PAGE]

X270/11/01

NATIONAL
QUALIFICATIONS
2012

WEDNESDAY, 16 MAY
1.00 PM – 2.00 PM

ENGLISH
INTERMEDIATE 2
Close Reading

Answer all questions.

30 marks are allocated to this paper.

Read the passage carefully and then answer **all** the questions, **using your own words as far as possible**.

The questions will ask you to show that:

you understand the main ideas and important details in the passage—in other words, **what** the writer has said (**Understanding—U**);

you can identify, using appropriate terms, the techniques the writer has used to get across these ideas—in other words, **how** he has said it (**Analysis—A**);

you can, using appropriate evidence, comment on how effective the writer has been—in other words, **how well** he has said it (**Evaluation—E**).

A code letter (U, A, E) is used alongside each question to identify its purpose for you. The number of marks attached to each question will give some indication of the length of answer required.

SUPERSTITION

In this passage, the writer explores how superstition can both help and hinder us.

Tennis players are a funny bunch. Have you noticed how they always ask for three balls instead of two; how they bounce the ball the same number of times before serving, as if any deviation from their routine might bring the world collapsing on their heads?

5 But the superstitions and rituals so beloved by the world's top players are not confined to the court. They take even more bizarre twists when the poor dears get home after their matches. Goran Ivanisevic got it into his head that if he won a match he had to repeat everything he did the previous day, such as eating the same food at the same restaurant, talking to the same people and watching the same TV programmes. One year this meant that he had to watch Teletubbies every morning during his Wimbledon

10 campaign. "Sometimes it got very boring," he said.

Could it be that these multifarious superstitions tell us something of deeper importance not only about humanity but about other species on the planet?

The answer, I think, is to be found in the world of pigeons. Yes, really. These feathered fellows, you see, are the tennis players of the bird world. Don't take my word for it:

15 that was the opinion of B. F. Skinner, the man widely regarded as the father of modern psychology.

Skinner's view was based on a groundbreaking experiment that he carried out in 1947 in which he placed some hungry pigeons in a cage attached to an automatic mechanism that delivered food "at regular intervals with no reference whatsoever to the bird's

20 behaviour". He discovered that the pigeons associated the delivery of the food with whatever chance actions they happened to be performing at the moment it was first delivered. So what did the pigeons do? They kept performing the same actions, even though they had no effect whatsoever on the release of food.

I know, I know. This is nothing compared with the weird behaviour that goes on

25 at Wimbledon, but do you see the connection? The pigeons were acting as if they could influence the mechanism delivering the Trill in just the same way that Ivanisevic thought that he could influence the outcome of his next match by watching Teletubbies. To put it a tad formally, they both witnessed a random connection between a particular kind of behaviour and a desired outcome, and then (wrongly) inferred that one caused

30 the other.

But did Ivanisevic really believe that his superstitions were effective or was he just having us on? Well, let's hear from the man himself – this is what he said when asked if he had ever abandoned a ritual when it stopped working: "I didn't. They do work. I won Wimbledon." So, he really did believe. And what of the pigeons? They were,

35 unfortunately, unavailable for interview.

Superstitious behaviour emerged quite early in evolutionary history. What is certain is that it is widespread, particularly within *homo sapiens*. More than half of Americans admitted to being superstitious in a recent poll, and it is not just silly and gullible types either. At Harvard University, students frequently rub the foot of the statue of John

40 Harvard for good luck.

Even cricketers, perhaps the brightest and most sensible sportsmen of all (well, that's what they tell us), are not immune to superstition. Jack Russell, the former England wicketkeeper, was among the most notorious, refusing to change his hat or wicketkeeping

pads throughout his career, even though they became threadbare and smelly, something
45 that really got up the noses of his team-mates.

But this raises another, deeper question: why do so many of us maintain rituals of
various kinds when they have no real connection with the desired outcome? Or, to put it
another way, why is superstitious behaviour so widespread, not just within our species
but beyond, when it seems to confer no tangible benefits? It's here that things get really
50 interesting (and just a little complex). And, as with most interesting things, the answer
is to be found in deep evolutionary history.

Imagine a caveman going to pick some berries from some bushes near his rocky abode.
He hears some rustling in the bushes and wrongly infers that there is a lion lurking in
there and scarpers. He even gets a little superstitious about those bushes and gives them
55 a wide berth in future. Is this superstition a problem to our caveman? Well, not if there
are plenty of other berry-bearing bushes from which to get his five-a-day.

But suppose that there really is a lion living in those bushes. The caveman's behaviour
now looks not only sensible but life-saving. So, a tendency to perceive connections that
do not actually exist can confer huge evolutionary benefits, providing a cocoon of safety
60 in a turbulent and dangerous world. The only proviso (according to some devilishly
complicated mathematics known as game theory) is this: your superstitions must not
impose too much of a burden on those occasions when they are without foundation.

And this is almost precisely what superstitions look like in the modern world. Some
believe in horoscopes, but few allow them to dictate their behaviour; some like to wear
65 the same lucky shoes to every job interview, but it is not as if wearing a different pair
would improve their chances of success; some like to bounce the ball precisely seven
times before serving at tennis, but although they are wrong to suppose that this ball-
bouncing is implicated in their success, it does not harm their prospects (even if it
irritates those of us watching).

70 It is only when a superstition begins to compromise our deeper goals and aspirations
that we have moved along the spectrum of irrationality far enough to risk a diagnosis of
obsessive compulsive disorder. Take Kolo Touré, the former Arsenal defender, who
insists on being the last player to leave the dressing room after the half-time break. No
real problem, you might think, except that when William Gallas, his team-mate, was
75 injured and needed treatment at half-time during a match, Touré stayed in the dressing
room until Gallas had been treated, forcing Arsenal to start the second half with only
nine players.

When a superstition that is supposed to help you actually hinders you, it is probably
time to kick the ritual into touch. With a rabbit's foot, obviously.

Matthew Syed, in *The Times*

QUESTIONS

Marks   Code

1. Look at lines 1–3, and then explain **in your own words** what is meant by
    tennis players being "a funny bunch".

    1   U

2. Consider the first two sentences of the second paragraph (lines 4–6), and
    then show how any example of the writer's **word choice** here reveals what
    his attitude to "top players" is.

    2   U

QUESTIONS (continued)

Marks Code

3. Explain why the paragraph in lines 11 and 12 works well at this point as a link of the ideas in the passage.

     2   A

4. Explain **in your own words** why the writer can fccl confident about using B. F. Skinner (see line 15) to support his claims about pigeons.

     1   U

5. Explain how effective you find the writer's use of the **image** or **metaphor** "groundbreaking" (line 17) to refer to Skinner's experiment.

     1   E

6. Look at lines 24–30, and then explain fully and **in your own words** what "the connection" was.

     3   U

7. What is the effect of the inclusion of the sentence "They were, unfortunately, unavailable for interview" (lines 34–35)?

     1   A

8. Why does the writer include the reference to Harvard University (line 39)?

     1   A

9. Explain the humour of "something that really got up the noses of his team-mates" (lines 44–45).

     2   A

10. Look again at lines 52–56.

    (a) How do these lines relate to the ideas the writer presents in the previous paragraph?

     2   A

    (b) What is surprising about the expression "to get his five-a-day" (line 56)?

     2   A

11. Explain **in your own words** what the "huge evolutionary benefits" (line 59) of superstitions are.

     2   U

12. Explain the writer's use of a colon in line 61.

     1   A

13. Look again at lines 63–69, in which the writer examines the nature of superstition nowadays.

    (a) Explain **in your own words** the points the writer makes.

     2   U

    (b) How does the **sentence structure** reinforce the ideas the writer is putting forward?

     1   A

14. Explain how effective you find the word "spectrum" (line 71) as an **image** or **metaphor** to illustrate people's "irrationality".

     2   E

15. Why does the writer include the anecdote about the footballer Kolo Touré (lines 72–77)?

     2   A

16. How effective do you find any aspect of the final paragraph (lines 78–79) as a conclusion to the passage?

    Your answer might deal with such features as **word choice** or **tone**.

     2   E

[END OF QUESTION PAPER]   **Total (30)**

X270/11/02

NATIONAL QUALIFICATIONS 2012	WEDNESDAY, 16 MAY 2.20 PM – 3.50 PM	ENGLISH INTERMEDIATE 2 Critical Essay

Answer **two** questions.

Each question must be taken from a different section.

Each question is worth 25 marks.

Answer TWO questions from this paper.

Each question must be chosen from a different Section (A–E). You are not allowed to choose two questions from the same Section.

In all Sections you may use Scottish texts.

Write the number of each question in the margin of your answer booklet and begin each essay on a fresh page.

You should spend about 45 minutes on each essay.

The following will be assessed:

- the relevance of your essays to the questions you have chosen

- your knowledge and understanding of key elements, central concerns and significant details of the chosen texts

- your explanation of ways in which aspects of structure/style/language contribute to the meaning/effect/impact of the chosen texts

- your evaluation of the effectiveness of the chosen texts, supported by detailed and relevant evidence

- the quality and technical accuracy of your writing.

Each question is worth 25 marks. The total for this paper is 50 marks.

SECTION A—DRAMA

Answers to questions in this section should refer to the text and to such relevant features as: characterisation, key scene(s), structure, climax, theme, plot, conflict, setting . . .

1. Choose a play in which there is conflict between two characters in a family **or** a group.

   Show how the conflict occurs and explain how it affects the characters and the events of the play.

2. Choose a play in which a main character's actions have a significant effect on the rest of the play.

   Show how this character's actions have affected the other characters **and/or** the outcome of the play.

3. Choose a play which has developed your understanding of an important human emotion such as love, hatred, jealousy **or** any other emotion.

   Show how this understanding has been developed through the playwright's use of dramatic techniques.

SECTION B—PROSE

> *Answers to questions in this section should refer to the text and to such relevant features as: characterisation, setting, language, key incident(s), climax, turning point, plot, structure, narrative technique, theme, ideas, description . . .*

4. Choose a novel **or** a short story where there is an incident which is a turning point crucial to the fate of the main character.

   Briefly describe what happens at this point and go on to explain why this is crucial to the fate of a main character.

5. Choose a novel **or** a short story in which setting in place **and/or** time is an important feature.

   Briefly describe the setting(s) and explain the importance of this feature to the story.

6. Choose a novel **or** a short story **or** a non-fiction text **or** group of texts which deals with an important human issue (such as the abuse of power, conflict between good and evil, loss of freedom or hatred between individuals or groups).

   Show how the author reveals the issue through the portrayal of people and events throughout the text, and show how your understanding of the issue has deepened.

SECTION C—POETRY

> *Answers to questions in this section should refer to the text and to such relevant features as: word choice, tone, imagery, structure, content, rhythm, theme, sound, ideas . . .*

7. Choose a poem which describes a person's experience.

   Explain how the poetic techniques used to describe the experience make the poem more interesting.

8. Choose a poem which arouses strong emotion in you.

   Describe how you feel about the poem, and explain how the poet leads you to feel this way.

9. Choose a poem in which the poet creates a particular mood **or** atmosphere.

   Show how the poet creates this mood **or** atmosphere by his or her choice of subject matter and use of poetic techniques.

[Turn over

SECTION D—FILM AND TV DRAMA

> *Answers to questions in this section should refer to the text and to such relevant features as: use of camera, key sequence, characterisation, mise-en-scène, editing, setting, music/sound, special effects, plot, dialogue . . .*

10. Choose a film **or** TV drama* in which the main character is an individual for whom we feel sympathy.

    Show how media techniques are used to portray the character in such a way that we feel sympathy.

11. Choose a scene or sequence from a film **or** TV drama* which is particularly dramatic.

    Describe what happens in the scene or sequence, explaining how the film or programme makers effectively use techniques to create drama.

12. Choose a film **or** TV drama* in which there is a character who poses a threat to the main character.

    Show how media techniques are used to portray the character in such a way that the audience reacts against him/her and sees the threat which he/she poses.

    * "TV drama" includes a single play, a series or a serial.

SECTION E—LANGUAGE

> *Answers to questions in this section should refer to the text and to such relevant features as: register, accent, dialect, slang, jargon, vocabulary, tone, abbreviation . . .*

13. Consider the language of advertisements aimed at young people.

    By discussing at least one such advertisement, identify the key features which vary from other types of advertising and explain why these features could appeal to young people.

14. Consider the language specific to a group with a shared hobby, job, interest **or** location.

    By giving examples of distinctive vocabulary **or** grammatical constructions, show how the group's language is different from that used by the general population and discuss the advantages to the group of using its specific language.

15. Consider the differences between written language and an aspect of spoken language which you have studied.

    Explain, with references to examples, the similarities and differences between the two forms of language you have studied and go on to show which features of spoken language you find most effective.

[END OF QUESTION PAPER]

[BLANK PAGE]

[BLANK PAGE]

**HODDER
GIBSON**
LEARN MORE

[BLANK PAGE]

X270/11/01

NATIONAL
QUALIFICATIONS
2013

FRIDAY, 17 MAY
1.00 PM – 2.00 PM

ENGLISH
INTERMEDIATE 2
Close Reading

Answer all questions.

30 marks are allocated to this paper.

Read the passage carefully and then answer **all** the questions, **using your own words as far as possible**.

The questions will ask you to show that:

> you understand the main ideas and important details in the passage—in other words, **what** the writer has said (**Understanding—U**);

> you can identify, using appropriate terms, the techniques the writer has used to get across these ideas—in other words, **how** he/she has said it (**Analysis—A**);

> you can, using appropriate evidence, comment on how effective the writer has been—in other words, **how well** he/she has said it (**Evaluation—E**).

A code letter (U, A, E) is used alongside each question to identify its purpose for you. The number of marks attached to each question will give some indication of the length of answer required.

WHY REALITY TV WORKS

In this passage, the writer explores some of the reasons for the popularity of reality TV shows such as "The X Factor".

It is a Saturday night in the northernmost fringes of London. Outside an anonymous building with blanked-out windows, a discarded plastic bag swirls in the breeze.

At first glance it seems a miserable place. But in fact this is where dreams are made and broken. Because this is where, every weekend, *The X Factor* goes live.

5 *The X Factor*, brainchild of Simon Cowell, is the most popular programme on Saturday night. Each week, hundreds make the pilgrimage to be part of the live audience, and millions of us tune in at home to watch.

As a result, many of us will spend more time in the virtual company of the contestants than we do with our real-life friends and family. In a modern world in which local
10 communities have become increasingly fractured, where relatives live further apart from each other than ever before and where one in five of us will never speak to our neighbours, Cowell's creation seems to be filling the void.

And yet despite the fact that more of us seem to be tuning in than ever before, relatively little is known about who watches and why. All we know is that *The X Factor*—whether
15 it signifies the reinvigoration of weekend family viewing or the disintegration of civilised society—is a reality-television phenomenon.

So why, after a decade of phone-in rows, vote-rigging accusations and celebrity-hungry wannabes with bloated egos, does the British public remain so in love with reality television?

20 By now most of us know that the version of reality on offer is one shaped by a multimillion-pound business with slick production values, and yet we willingly suspend our disbelief week after week, month after month, in the name of entertainment. Is there something lacking in our daily lives that draws us so inexorably into Cowell's web?

We do get swept up in it, wanting to be behind somebody, wanting them to do well.
25 That's why producers will make the hard-luck story—those little snippets of someone struggling in a dead-end job—because that enables us to feel we have a sort of connection.

And perhaps, in a world increasingly dominated by Facebook and Twitter, where friendships are made and broken at the click of the computer mouse, we feel more comfortable engaging with someone on the other side of the screen rather than chatting
30 to them over the garden fence, as our grandparents might once have done. If we are already sharing the details of our private lives in Tweets and status updates, are we also becoming more accustomed to the notion of putting our intimate selves on display for the entertainment of others?

It's no coincidence that our love affair with *The X Factor* is so potent right now, more
35 than ever before, as Britain endures a period of relative austerity. In a time of economic hardship, we are seeking out the simple and cheap—family entertainment that makes us feel part of something bigger. But the popularity of such shows may be traced back even further—to the emergence of 19th-century periodicals which relied on reader contributions. Reality TV is merely a manifestation of a very, very old craving. We
40 love sentimental stories, such as Dickens' Little Nell; we love a tear jerker, and shows like *The X Factor* are no more crass or exploitative than cheap sensational 19th-century fiction.

Yet it seems that 21st-century viewers are looking for more than just simple entertainment. Part of the attraction is the sense of control *The X Factor* gives us: the sense that we

45 can put right wider social wrongs by voting for our favourite contestants and that although our lives are being shaped by forces beyond our control—such as government cutbacks, widespread job losses or social deprivation—the ability to have a say in what happens to others in reality TV shows gives us back a much-needed sense of power.

The most popular contestants almost always have a backstory of personal triumph over
50 adversity which enables us to feel that we are helping them succeed, that we are giving them a break even if no one else will. And perhaps this is why Susan Boyle, who grew up in a council house and was bullied as a child for her learning difficulties, has proved such an enduring figure.

Of course there are less noble motivations for watching, too: for every Susan Boyle there
55 is a caterwauling teenager who cannot hold a tune and yet remains convinced he or she is destined for stardom. A part of us just loves it when people are awful and embarrass themselves—but human nature is contradictory like that, and reality television allows us to have it both ways.

In fact, most of us know we are being manipulated and that our emotional buttons
60 are being shamelessly pressed every time there is a lingering close-up of a tear-stained contestant's face recounting the traumatic time their grandmother's budgerigar died. But because we have become so accustomed to such televisual shorthand, we are increasingly willing participants in the charade. We become, along with the contestants, part of the performance.

65 Do we care that reality television is not actually real? That question misses the point. Reality television is a completely constructed premise. None of the people would be in it if we were just showing their normal lives. But what it does do is take human flesh and blood and challenges it in situations that bring out a person's true personality. That's why shows work, because the public is after authenticity . . . They want to support
70 people with talent and for them to win, but they punish pretension and two-facedness. On the whole, the public are positive, but they are judgemental.

Perhaps this, in the end, is the key to Cowell's success: he acknowledges that we crave the appearance of reality, but that we also want the reassurance of a happy ending for those who deserve it and retribution for those who do not.

75 Either that or we just want to laugh at the man with the comb-over singing an out-of-tune Mariah Carey song.

Adapted from an article by
Elizabeth Day, in The Observer

QUESTIONS

Marks Code

1. Explain why any **one** example of the writer's **word choice** from paragraph 1 (lines 1–2) helps to give the impression that the place she describes is "miserable".
1   U/A

2. Explain how effective you find the expression "pilgrimage" (line 6) as an **image** or **metaphor**.
2   E

3. (a) Show how another expression in the immediate context helps us understand the meaning of "virtual" (line 8).
2   U

  (b) Explain **in your own words one** of the reasons why there is a "void" which "Cowell's creation seems to be filling" (line 12).
2   U

QUESTIONS (continued)   *Marks*   *Code*

4. Explain **fully** why any **two** components of the expression "celebrity-hungry wannabes with bloated egos" (lines 17–18) convey a **tone** of disapproval.   2   A

5. Look at lines 20–23, and then explain what is suggested by the writer's **word choice** of **either** "slick" **or** "web".   1   U

6. Explain **fully** the function of the words in dashes (the parenthesis) in lines 25–26.   2   A

7. Look at lines 27–33, and then

   (*a*) explain **in your own words** what is meant by "engaging with someone on the other side of the screen";   2   U

   (*b*) explain **in your own words** why people do this;   1   U

   (*c*) explain how well the **content** of the sentence beginning "If we are" reinforces the writer's argument;   2   E

   (*d*) identify an aspect of the **structure** of this sentence which helps the writer get the content across.   1   A

8. Look at lines 34–42, and then explain **in your own words two** reasons the writer gives in this paragraph for "our love affair with *The X Factor*".   2   U

9. Explain **fully** why the sentence "Yet it seems that 21st-century viewers are looking for more than just simple entertainment." (line 43) works well as a link at this point in the passage.   2   A

10. Re-read lines 43–53, and then explain **in your own words** why the writer chooses Susan Boyle as an example to support her argument.   2   A

11. Look at lines 54–58, and then explain how the writer achieves a wry or humorous **tone** in these lines.   2   A

12. The word "charade" (line 63) usually refers to a pretence, something that is false or fake.

    Explain how an expression used by the writer earlier in this paragraph prepares us for the word "charade".   2   U/A

13. Look at the last two paragraphs (lines 72–76), and then explain how they help to provide an effective conclusion to the passage.

    You may wish to consider such aspects as **word choice**, **ideas**, **structure** and/or **tone**.   2   A/E

Total (30)

[END OF QUESTION PAPER]

[Open out for Questions]

[BLANK PAGE]

X270/11/02

NATIONAL QUALIFICATIONS 2013	FRIDAY, 17 MAY 2.20 PM – 3.50 PM	**ENGLISH** INTERMEDIATE 2 Critical Essay

Answer **two** questions.

Each question must be taken from a different section.

Each question is worth 25 marks.

Answer TWO questions from this paper.

Each question must be chosen from a different Section (A–E). You are not allowed to choose two questions from the same Section.

In all Sections you may use Scottish texts.

Write the number of each question in the margin of your answer booklet and begin each essay on a fresh page.

You should spend about 45 minutes on each essay.

The following will be assessed:

- **the relevance of your essays to the questions you have chosen**

- **your knowledge and understanding of key elements, central concerns and significant details of the chosen texts**

- **your explanation of ways in which aspects of structure/style/language contribute to the meaning/effect/impact of the chosen texts**

- **your evaluation of the effectiveness of the chosen texts, supported by detailed and relevant evidence**

- **the quality and technical accuracy of your writing.**

Each question is worth 25 marks. The total for this paper is 50 marks.

SECTION A—DRAMA

Answers to questions in this section should refer to the text and to such relevant features as: characterisation, key scene(s), structure, climax, theme, plot, conflict, setting . . .

1.   Choose a play in which the breakdown of a relationship between main characters is an important feature.

Discuss the cause(s) of the breakdown and show how it goes on to have a significant impact on the rest of the play.

2.   Choose a play which deals with an important human issue.

State what the issue is and explain how **one or more** of the characters in the play deal with it.

3.   Choose a play in which there is a scene which could be described as a turning point in the fate of **one or more** of the characters.

Show how this scene could be described as a turning point and explain how it increased your understanding of the character or the characters in the rest of the play.

SECTION B—PROSE

Answers to questions in this section should refer to the text and to such relevant features as: characterisation, setting, language, key incident(s), climax, turning point, plot, structure, narrative technique, theme, ideas, description . . .

4. Choose a novel **or** a short story in which there is conflict between **two** characters.

   Examine the nature of the conflict and explain to what extent it is resolved.

5. Choose a novel **or** a short story with a message which is still relevant today.

   Show how the author's portrayal of events and character(s) highlight the author's message.

6. Choose a novel **or** a short story **or** a non-fiction text **or** group of texts which made a strong impact on you.

   Explain how the writer's use of language creates this impact.

SECTION C—POETRY

Answers to questions in this section should refer to the text and to such relevant features as: word choice, tone, imagery, structure, content, rhythm, theme, sound, ideas . . .

7. Choose a poem which describes a place **or** an incident.

   Briefly state where **or** what is being described, and go on to explain how the techniques used in the poem make the description memorable.

8. Choose a poem which takes a particular form, such as sonnet, ode, ballad, elegy, monologue …

   Explain how the distinctive features of this form contribute to your appreciation of the poem.

9. Choose a poem which has an ending which you found surprising **or** interesting **or** satisfying **or** inspiring.

   Consider the whole poem, and by reference to the poet's use of content and poetic techniques explain why you think the ending is particularly effective.

[Turn over

SECTION D—FILM AND TV DRAMA

> *Answers to questions in this section should refer to the text and to such relevant features as:* use of camera, key sequence, characterisation, mise-en-scène, editing, setting, music/sound, special effects, plot, dialogue . . .

10. Choose a film **or** TV drama* where conflict between characters is central to the plot.

    Explain the reasons for the conflict and show how media techniques intensify audience involvement at particular scenes.

11. Choose a film which is an example of a specific genre such as horror, romance, action or comedy.

    Explain how the film makers have used the features of the genre to create a successful film.

12. Choose a film **or** TV drama* which highlights a particular moral **or** political **or** social **or** environmental issue.

    Identify the issue and show how media techniques are used to persuade us to adopt a particular view or to explore the issue more fully.

    * "TV drama" includes a single play, a series or a serial.

SECTION E—LANGUAGE

> *Answers to questions in this section should refer to the text and to such relevant features as:* register, accent, dialect, slang, jargon, vocabulary, tone, abbreviation . . .

13. Consider the use of persuasive techniques in a series of advertisements run in newspapers or magazines, television, radio, the internet or in public spaces.

    Show how the persuasive techniques have been built up over the series, and explain how such features are successful in helping to sell the product.

14. Consider features of language which help to give a particular group of people a strong sense of identity, **or** belonging, **or** tradition.

    Explain what some of the key features of your chosen language are and go on to show in what ways this language is so important to your chosen group.

15. Choose an aspect of communication (television, radio, internet etc) which you feel has recently made an impact on every day language in either a positive **or** a negative way.

    Explain what you consider the key areas of impact to be and show how negative **or** positive this impact has been.

[END OF QUESTION PAPER]

[BLANK PAGE]

Acknowledgements

Permission has been sought from all relevant copyright holders and Hodder Gibson is grateful for the use of the following:

An extract adapted from an article by Carol Lee in 'The Times', 10th June 2006, from her book 'A Child Called Freedom' (Thistle e-book). (2009 Close Reading pages 2–3);

An extract from the article 'China's Colossus' by Damian Whitworth taken from 'The Times' © The Times/NI Syndication, 30th August 2007 (2010 Close Reading pages 2–3);

An extract from the article '2b or not 2b' by David Crystal from 'The Guardian', 5th June 2008. Originally from 'txtng: the gr8 db8' published by Oxford University Press, 2008 © David Crystal (2011 Close Reading pages 2–3);

The article 'Superstition' by Matthew Syed © The Times/NI Syndication, 1st July 2009 (2012 Close Reading pages 2–3);

The article 'Reality Check' by Elizabeth Day taken from 'The Observer Magazine', 21st November 2010. Copyright Guardian News & Media Ltd 2010 (2013 Close Reading pages 2–3).

SQA INTERMEDIATE 2
ENGLISH 2009–2013

ENGLISH INTERMEDIATE 2
CLOSE READING
2009

1. *Any one: quotation/reference, comment from:*
   The bluntness/brevity/content of the opening sentence; "hundreds of others" is emphasised by use of parenthesis; the use of the colon isolates or enforces the pause before "Soweto"; the positioning of "Soweto" gives a climactic effect

2. Uprising: "took to the streets"/"march"/"(in) protest"
   Oppression: "(under the) apartheid regime" (or "apartheid" or "regime" alone) or "opened fire"

3. (a) A Government rule/law/decree/statute/order (gloss of "edict") forcing teaching in Afrikaans/making it obligatory/enforced/required (gloss of "compulsory")

   (b) It was a threat to their self-esteem or identity (gloss of "unpeople")
   OR it was a threat to their (intellectual) independence (gloss of "thinking for themselves")
   OR it was the last straw (gloss of "the last of a line of insults")

4. (a) They were abiding/memorable/lasting/ageless
   OR they were masterpieces (gloss of "classics")
   OR the regime did not understand their content (gloss of "didn't know what was in these books")

   (b) *Any one from:*
   They identified with Oliver and/or the events portrayed in the book/
   Their lives were like/the same as Oliver's
   Because they too were subjugated/exploited (gloss of "oppression" or "slave labour")
   OR they too were underfed (gloss of "hungry" or "thin rations")
   OR the inference can be made that they too were in poor health (gloss of "frail")
   OR they too were brave (gloss of "courageous")
   OR they too were mocked (by oppressors) (gloss of "cruel taunts")

5. To complement or convey the idea of surprise or ridicule.

6. (a) "books" refers back to Dickens in previous paragraph ; "not enough" anticipates the idea of paucity/scarcity developed in the rest of the paragraph

   (b) The exact figures/"1500 pupils and three copies"/"waiting months for their turn" shows the contrast between demand and supply

7. A reward is normally pleasant but what happened to them was unpleasant
   OR
   What happened to them was unpleasant
   and so the term is incongruous/peculiar/strange/odd/poignant/sarcastic/sardonic

8. The references to the unfairness/brutality/ unattractiveness (addressing the idea of ugliness) and (brave) resistance (addressing the idea of being "nothing daunted"); (clearly) show (why the Africans felt) Dickens was on their side

9. He showed that pain/distress/misery/anguish (gloss of "suffering") was the same throughout the world/in all places/the world over (gloss of "everywhere")

10. They taught them by word of mouth (gloss of "orally") and then drove/pushed/encouraged (gloss of "urged") them to read.

11. The long and short sentences contrast
    OR the dash produces a (dramatic) delay
    OR the brevity of the second sentence produces impact
    OR the introduction of the second sentence with "And" produces impact

12. Just as drugs are harmful (in the long term) so Afrikaans has a (long-reaching) deleterious effect on the lives of the Sowetans

13. Answers must identify one aspect or feature of the final paragraph and link it to a relevant aspect or feature elsewhere in the passage eg
    There is recapitulation of previously-mentioned ideas such as that of Dickens being long dead
    There is relation back to the introductory 3 paragraphs in the reference to Afrikaans
    There is relation back to the introductory 2 paragraphs in the reference to the date
    There is a reprising of an idea in the opening in the reference to the death of Hector Pieterson
    There is recapitulation of the idea of optimism in the uplifting tone

ENGLISH INTERMEDIATE 2
CRITICAL ESSAY
2009

Please see Critical Essay Marking Principles on page 72.

ENGLISH INTERMEDIATE 2
CLOSE READING
2010

1. He had never/barely heard of him/puzzlement

2.

Question (and response) Verbless sentence(s) (throwaway effect of)"of course" Informality of abbreviated verbs (Helpful) explanation of pronunciation Use of 2nd person Humour of (facetious) capital letter at "Who" Informal use of initial "But" Terminal preposition ("about")	Makes it more informal/friendlier/less intimidating OR is a feature of conversation/ dialogue/ engagement

3. *Any two from:*
   He is a very important person in history (gloss of "colossal" or "greatest");
   He set up/founded China (gloss of "created");
   He set up/founded an imperial dynasty (gloss of "First Emperor");
   His regime was the most permanent/durable/ prolonged (gloss of "long-lasting")

4.

Example	Analysis
changed the world	suggests large extent of influence
terribly few	conveys near-uniqueness
(whose achievements) lasted like that	suggests permanence of influence
Really	intensifies
"great"	shows attitude of high regard
repetition of "great, great"	emphasises

5. *Any two from:*
   Glosses of:

stability	eg firmness/solidity/ strength/steadiness/ balance
durability	eg toughness/long-lasting quality/sturdiness/ resilience
chariots could ride relatively smoothly (down the same ruts in the road)	eg progress (in channels/grooves/ furrows) was easy/easier
avoid churning up the entire highway	eg road was not made uneven/less smooth/harder to make progress on/not so damaged

6. It (neatly/succinctly) continues/sums up/reinforces/emphasises/alludes to the frightening/redoubtable/fearsome quality and the efficiency/competence/ruthlessness of the army

7. *Any two from:*
   Glosses of:

surveillance culture/spy	people watched/observed one another
terrible punishments	severe reprisals/penalties
Many laws	multiplicity of regulations/edicts/ rulings/instructions

8. It conveys the hardship/protractedness/drudgery of the work

9. (*a*) It represents/stands for/is (readily) recognisable as representative (of China)

   (*b*)

Gloss of "historical" or "age-old"	eg long-standing
Gloss of "separateness"	eg isolation
Gloss of "industriousness"	eg capacity for hard work

10. "establishing complete control over his empire" refers back to preceding ideas (relating to dominance)
    "was not enough" prepares us for upcoming reference (to other things he wanted to do or have)
    "But" introduces contrast

11. *Any two points from:*
    He uses "may"; twice; he uses "some archaeologists" he uses "hope"; he uses "one day"; he uses "some form"

12.

Content	He refers to the large number of people involved in its construction OR the large number of pits OR the large number of artefacts found OR the possibility of many more OR the desire to have many servants etc. (paraphrase of last sentence) Generalised comment about large numbers acceptable
Technique	
Typography	he uses numerals (for impact)
Word choice	he uses "empire", which suggests size of construction OR he uses "army", which alludes to the large numbers of figures

One answer from each section needed for 2 marks

13.

word choice	"I can't think of anyone else"	(emphatically) conveys sense of uniqueness
	"scale of ambition"	(clearly) conveys size of imagination/ grandeur of plan
	"entire kingdom"	(clearly) conveys size of undertaking
	"Nobody else (in human history has attempted to do that)"	(emphatically) conveys sense of uniqueness/rareness
	"fascinating"	(clearly) suggests the captivating nature of (this aspect of) the story
structure	repetition of "anyone/ nobody else"	(clearly) emphasises uniqueness
	repetition of "we have no"	(clearly) emphasises uniqueness

One mark for feature, one for evaluative comment

14. Unusual/unconventional/strange/ironic/quaint/ peculiar

15. *Any one example and explanation from:*

"mass ranks"	recapitulates idea of large numbers
"Terracotta Army"	returns to an expression used in opening paragraph
"(breathtaking) megalomania"	recapitulates ideas/word used earlier
"wonders of the world"	recapitulates idea of magnificence
"(The telling of that story is long) overdue"	recapitulates idea of undeserved anonymity

ENGLISH INTERMEDIATE 2
CRITICAL ESSAY
2010

Please see Critical Essay Marking Principles on page 72.

ENGLISH INTERMEDIATE 2
CLOSE READING
2011

1. (a) Any of "vandals", "(what) Genghis Khan (did to his neighbours)", "destroying", "pillaging", "savaging"

   (b) Idea of alliteration
   or similarity / balance of construction
   e.g. both three-word phrases, both participial phrases, both containing "our"
   or
   identification of (humorous effect of) hyperbole

2.

textese	suffix "–ese" is pejorative
slanguage	(portmanteau) inclusion of "slang" is denigratory
virus	(metaphor) suggests destructiveness / disease / being harmful or unwanted
bleak	suggests (e.g.) poverty of language
bald	suggests (e.g.) plainness of language
sad	suggests regret about development or (more colloquial sense of) inadequacy
drab	suggests (e.g.) dreariness / monotony of language
shrinktalk	suggests impoverishment or (Orwellian) connotation of "-talk" suffix
masks	suggests (unwelcome) concealment of (unpalatable) truth

3. They are examples of "(new) technology" / mediums of communication which was/were originally unwanted / (needlessly) frightened people / proved to be non-harmful / beneficial

   answers also acceptable which refer to the historical progression showing it is a repeated phenomenon

4. (a) They were varied / differing / contrasting / controversial / intense

   (b) *Word choice:*
   • Comment may be on
   • the varied / contradictory nature of words used: NB comment, not mere identification (may be exemplified, e.g. opposing nature of "antagonism" and "enthusiasm")
   • **or** "such" suggesting intensity of reactions
   • **or** "phenomenon" suggests (e.g.) social concern
   • **or** "all at once" suggests disturbing / contradictory nature of reactions

   Structure:
   • comment will be on **list** suggesting multiplicity or **question** being rhetorical or inviting agreement – must be more than mere identification of feature

5. *Any two from:*

Contradiction of "its distinctiveness is not a new phenomenon"	eg (the language) being different is new-fangled/modern/recent
Contradiction of "its use [is] restricted to the young"	eg only children/juveniles/teenagers use it
Contradiction of "it helps rather than hinders literacy"	eg it impedes/restricts/obstructs linguistic/verbal competence
Contradiction of "its long-term impact is negligible"	eg it will have a significant effect
Contradiction of "it is not a disaster"	eg it is a tragedy

6. Just as "hysteria" suggests panic / extremity / irrationality
   So the reaction to (innovative) text message language has been excessive / needless / illogical

7. He uses "stories", "reports", "no one was ever able to track down the entire essay"
   and "(probably a) hoax", "quoted incessantly"
   or
   quotation of one of these and comment on its contribution to the sense of untruth and/or credulousness
   or
   he tells the (apocryphal) essay story / gives an example to show what people were willing to believe

8. Both are acronyms / formed from initial letters / abbreviations.

9. Glosses of **two** of "English has had abbreviated words ever since it began to be written down" – eg this is not new/has a long history
   And "attracted criticism" or "complained" – eg have always had a hostile reception/met with disapproval
   And "have effectively become new words" – eg have been accepted into the language in their own right

10. They are proof of his point
    about literary respectability/long history of deviant forms
    or
    An assertion that the candidate has no/little idea who these people are
    And so this does not help his argument/make anything clear

11. The letters which are used most often (gloss of "frequently occurring")
    are not the most easily/most quickly written (gloss of "access" or "input")

12. "Abbreviations" or "(intuitive) response" introduces/points **forward** (to the contractions/reactions covered in the remainder of the paragraph); "technological problem" refers **back** (to the difficulties of entering letters mentioned in the previous paragraph)

13. It signals or introduces a contrast / contributes to a link
    Between the practical/technical reasons behind aspects of text language (he has been examining)
    And the other (psychological) ones (he goes on to explore)

14. Doubt/disagreement/cynicism/contention/irony/sarcasm

15. Knowledge about/sensitivity to language

16. Answers must relate some aspect of this paragraph to another feature or idea mentioned or used earlier in the passage

Aspect from last paragraph	*Reference to elsewhere*
Idea of dislike of or bemusement at texting	repeats idea of aversion mentioned in eg opening paragraphs.
Idea of creativity or adaptability	repeats idea of flexibility of language, in eg its not being a new phenomenon.
"There is no disaster pending"	echoes reassurances given elsewhere, eg in "it is not a disaster".
"We will not see a new generation of adults growing up unable to write proper English"/"The language as a whole will not decline"	repeats idea of children's linguistic awareness.
"texting…is language in evolution"	repeats idea of development mentioned elsewhere, eg in adoption of new abbreviated forms.
Upbeat, positive tone of last paragraph	echoes optimistic, affirmative tone throughout the passage (may be exemplified).

ENGLISH INTERMEDIATE 2 CRITICAL ESSAY 2011

Please see Critical Essay Marking Principles on page 72.

ENGLISH INTERMEDIATE 2
CLOSE READING
2012

1. odd/strange/curious/eccentric – ie not comical/amusing

2. Any one of "beloved", "bizarre", "twists" or "(poor) dears"
   suggests (e.g.) amusement/condescension/wonderment/lack of
   sympathy/mockery
   or
   any other acceptable comment **on the chosen example**

3. "(these multifarious) superstitions" or "(not only about)
   humanity" looks back to the ideas of the first two paragraphs
   "of deeper importance" anticipates more serious ideas which
   follow
   or
   "other species" anticipates following ideas (about pigeons)
   or
   "not only (about humanity)" signals a diversion
   or
   the question the sentence asks is then answered

4. Glosses of "widely regarded" (e.g. seen by many people/well-
   known/respected) or "father (of modern psychology)" (e.g. an
   innovative/authoritative figure)
   or
   Skinner used pigeons in his experiments

5. It (clearly) conveys the innovative nature of the experiment/he
   was doing something new
   or
   the expression may be perceived as a cliché

6. Both the pigeons and the tennis player (wrongly) thought their
   actions were linked to the consequences

7. It adds/contributes to the humour/sceptical tone of the passage

8. (To show that) intelligent people can be superstitious too/
   superstition is not just the preserve of "the silly and gullible"

9. There is the (literal) sense of being malodorous and the
   (figurative) sense of being annoying
   or
   The pun/double meaning/play on words of (literal and
   figurative) senses of being malodorous and being annoying

10. (*a*) They give an example/provide an illustration which
       addresses the reason(s) for superstition/continues the idea
       of "deep evolutionary history"

    (*b*) This is a modern/idealistic notion
       In a very old/more brutal context
       Condensed answer explaining incongruity/anachronism

11. Gloss of "providing a cocoon of safety in a turbulent and
    dangerous world": e.g. they insulate/shield/shelter/protect in
    unstable/risky/perilous/unsettled circumstances
    or
    gloss of "The caveman's behaviour now looks not only
    sensible but life-saving" e.g. being superstitious can make you
    cautious and (therefore) more likely to survive

12. It introduces an expansion or explanation (of what the
    "proviso" is).

13. (*a*) People (still) indulge in superstition (in various situations)
       But it has little influence/(beneficial) effect/is harmless

    (*b*) Idea of similarity of construction/repetition/triplet of
       "some… but"
       or
       comparability of relationship indicated/implied by use of
       semi-colons (N.B. not identification of semi-colon alone)

14.

It is appropriate because	Just as a spectrum contains a whole range/variety/scale (of colours)	so there is a (wide) range of superstitions/ (illogical) behaviours/ perceptions/beliefs
It is inappropriate because	the (bright) colour imagery implied	is not apt or fitting or helpful to describe/illustrate the (melancholy) subject

15. It illustrates his point about the range of "irrationality" by
    providing an extreme example of superstition
    or
    It illustrates his point that superstition taken to excess/
    dogmatically insisted upon has an unhelpful/deleterious
    effect/outcome
    or
    He is using reference to a team game to show the influence of
    superstition on others
    or
    He is using someone famous to help the reader connect

16. The reference to the elements of help and hindrance (neatly)
    recaps the idea of ambivalence explored elsewhere in the
    passage
    or
    "ritual" (tellingly) repeats a (significant) word used
    earlier/repeated (three times) earlier in the passage
    or
    (metaphor) "kick (the ritual into touch)" (neatly) reprises
    references to football/sport used earlier
    or
    "a rabbit's foot" is (clearly) associated with superstition which
    is the article's topic
    or
    "With a rabbit's foot, obviously" (adroitly) reprises the
    cynical/sceptical/humorous tone seen elsewhere

ENGLISH INTERMEDIATE 2
CRITICAL ESSAY
2012

Please see Critical Essay Marking Principles on page 72.

ENGLISH INTERMEDIATE 2
CLOSE READING
2013

1. *Any one from:*

"fringes"	suggests peripheral / marginalised quality
"anonymous building"	suggests lack of distinction
"blanked-out windows"	suggests (eg) fortress-like quality/ anonymity / facelessness / desolation
"discarded plastic bag"	suggests ugliness / neglect / lack of concern for environment
"swirls in the breeze"	suggests windiness / cheerlessness / neglect

2.

Just as a pilgrimage...	So attendance at The X Factor...
involves travel	involves going away
is / can be carried out by many	involves / can involve numbers
is done for devotional reasons	is done by devotees
gives pleasure	gives happiness

3. *(a)*

Retrieval of "real-life"	means the exact opposite (ie not actual / simulated / giving the appearance of)
or "tune in at home"	suggests technology-generated

(b)

Gloss of	
"local communities have become increasingly fractured" **or** "where relatives live further apart from each other than ever before" **or** "one in five of us will never speak to our neighbours"	eg neighbourhoods / districts are (ever more) split / separated / disjointed
	eg members of families are (physically) distant / far away from one another
	eg 20% / one fifth / a (significant) number of us have no communication with people next door / in vicinity

4. *Any two from:*

"celebrity-hungry"	suggests superficiality **or** indulgence / excessive ambition
"wannabes"	suggests inadequacy **or** is derogatory
"bloated"	suggests excess
"egos"	suggests self-fixation / arrogance

5. Slick: efficient / polished or deceptive
Web: predation / entrapment / sinister quality / all-embracing quality

6. They are an example of what could be a "hard-luck story"

7. *(a)* Glosses of "engaging" and "screen",
eg having a (perceived / imagined) relationship / connecting / chatting with people who appear on TV / by means of a computer link / over the Internet

(b) Gloss of "more comfortable", eg they prefer communicating this way / feel at ease / relaxed / secure
or
Reference to a "world increasingly dominated by Facebook and Twitter" or "at the click of the computer mouse" – eg this is a computer-focused / dependent age.

(c) It (clearly / validly / appropriately) makes a connection between (the increasing prominence of) "sharing the details of our private lives" (on-line social networking) and "putting our intimate selves on display" (reality TV)
or
gives the examples of Tweets or status updates to show how we are sharing ourselves publicly

(d) (Rhetorical) question or balance

8. Glosses of *Any two from:*

(because of) "austerity", "economic hardship"	eg we are hard up
("we are seeking") [the] "simple"	eg we want uncomplicated / undemanding / straightforward material
("we are seeking") "cheap"	eg we want material which does not cost much / is inexpensive / low-cost
("we are seeking") "family entertainment"	eg can be watched by everyone
"craving" for "sentimental stories" and "tear jerker"	eg we like (over -) emotional / slushy / maudlin entertainment
"part of something bigger"	eg gives feeling of involvement
"(manifestation of) a very, very old craving" or "19th-century fiction"	eg this is just another form of a basic or long-standing human characteristic

9. "simple entertainment" looks back (to previous paragraph's content)
   "(looking for) more (than)" looks forward (to additional points raised about control in the remainder of the paragraph)
   or
   "simple entertainment" looks back to previous paragraph's content (specified, eg "simple" or "cheap … 19th-century fiction")
   "(looking for) more (than)" looks forward to additional points raised about control / having a say / sense of power in the remainder of the paragraph

10. She represents / the reader can relate to triumph over injustice (gloss of "social wrongs") or hardship (gloss of "social deprivation")
    or
    The example of her success shows that the voter can redress injustice (gloss of "we can put right wider social wrongs")

11. Answers may address the writer's selection of content indicating incompetence and delusion eg someone who is "caterwauling" or "cannot hold a tune" (cannot sing) being convinced that he is "destined for stardom" (fame is beckoning)
    or
    reference to "caterwauling and extrapolation eg the suggestion that this (hyperbolically) illustrates the poor quality of the voice
    or
    Address the writer's selection of "a part of us just loves it when people are awful and embarrass themselves"
    eg we relish other people's disasters.

12.

"manipulated" or "our emotional buttons are being shamelessly pressed" or "lingering close-up of a tear stained contestant's face"	suggests control by others / exploitation
or "the traumatic time their grandmother's budgerigar died"	suggests excessive / maudlin reaction (to less significant event)

13. *Examples such as:*

"in the end" **or**	provides a signal of conclusion
"crave" **or**	repeats of word / idea used earlier
"the key to Cowell's success" **or**	recapitulates a focus of the passage
"the appearance of reality" **or**	recapitulates a central concern of the passage revisits ideas used earlier
"happy ending for those who deserve it and retribution for those who do not" **or** "laugh at the man with the comb-over singing out-of-tune"	repeats idea of technical incompetence or delusion

ENGLISH INTERMEDIATE 2 CRITICAL ESSAY 2013

Please see Critical Essay Marking Principles on page 72.

ENGLISH INTERMEDIATE 2
CRITICAL ESSAY
2009 TO 2013 EXAMS

Marking Principles for the Critical Essay are as follows:

- The essay should first be read to establish whether the essay achieves success in **all** the Performance Criteria for Grade C, including relevance and the standards for technical accuracy outlined in Note 1 below.
- If minimum standards are not achieved in any **one** or more of the Performance Criteria, the maximum mark which can be awarded is 11.
- If minimum standards have been achieved, then the supplementary marking grids will allow you to place the work on a scale of marks out of 25.
- The Category awarded and the mark should be placed at the end of the essay.

Notes:

1. "Sufficiently accurate" can best be defined in terms of a definition of "consistently accurate".

   - *Consistently accurate*
     A few errors may be present, but these will not be significant in any way. The candidate may use some complex vocabulary and sentence structures. Where appropriate, sentences will show accurate handling of clauses. Linking between sentences will be clear. Paragraphing will reflect a developing line of thought.

   - *Sufficiently accurate*
     As above but with an allowance made for speed and the lack of opportunity to redraft.

2. Using the Category descriptions

   - Categories are not grades. Although derived from performance criteria at C and the indicators of excellence for Grade A, the four categories are designed primarily to assist with placing each candidate response at an appropriate point on a continuum of achievement. Assumptions about final grades or association of final grades with particular categories should not be allowed to influence objective assessment.

   - Once an essay has been deemed to pass the basic criteria, it does not have to meet all the suggestions for Category II (for example) to fall into that Category. More typically there will be a spectrum of strengths and weaknesses which span categories.

GRADE C
Performance Criteria

(*a*) *Understanding*
   As appropriate to task, the response demonstrates understanding of key elements, central concerns and significant details of the text(s).

(*b*) *Analysis*
   The response explains in some detail ways in which aspects of structure/style/language contribute to meaning/effect/impact.

(*c*) *Evaluation*
   The response reveals engagement with the text(s) or aspects of the text(s) and stated or implied evaluation of effectiveness, substantiated by some relevant evidence from the text(s).

(*d*) *Expression*
   Structure, style and language, including use of some appropriate critical terminology, are deployed to communicate meaning clearly and develop a line of thought which is generally relevant to purpose; spelling, grammar and punctuation are sufficiently accurate.

It should be noted that the term "text" encompasses printed, audio or film/video text(s) which may be literary (fiction or non-fiction) or may relate to aspects of media or language.

Language Questions 13 - 15

- The "text" which should be dealt with in a language question is the research which the pupil has done. Examples taken from their research must be there for you to see.
- However, to demonstrate understanding and analysis related to these examples there has to be some ability to generalise from the particular, to classify and comment on what has been discovered. It is not enough merely to produce a list of words in, say, Dundonian with their standard English equivalents. This is merely description and without any further development does not demonstrate understanding of any principle underlying the choice of words.
- The list of features at the head of the section is supportive. A marker would reasonably expect that some such features would be mentioned in the course of the candidate's answer.

Intermediate 2 Critical Essay Supplementary Advice

This advice, which is supplementary to the published Performance Criteria, is designed to assist with the placing of scripts within the full range of marks. However, the Performance Criteria as published give the primary definitions. The mark range for each Category is identified.

IV 8–11	III 12–15	II 16–19	I 20–25
• An essay which falls into this category may do so for a variety of reasons. It could be • that it fails to achieve sufficient technical accuracy • or that any knowledge and understanding of the material is not deployed as a response relevant to the task • or that analysis and evaluation attempted are unconvincing • or that the answer is simply too thin.	**Understanding** • Knowledge of the text(s), and a basic understanding of the **main** concerns will be used .... to provide an answer which is **generally relevant** to the task. • Some reference to the text(s) will be made to **support** the candidate's argument.	**Understanding** • Knowledge and understanding of the **central** concerns of the text(s) will be used .... to provide an answer which is **mainly relevant** to the task. • Reference to the text(s) will be used as evidence to **promote** the candidate's argument.	**Understanding** • **Secure** knowledge **and some insight** into the central concerns of the text(s) will be demonstrated at this level .... and there will be a line of thought which is **consistently relevant** to the task. • Reference to the text(s) will be used **appropriately** as evidence which helps to **develop** the argument **fully**.
	Analysis • There will be an **explanation** of the contribution of literary/linguistic techniques to the impact of the text(s).	**Analysis** • There will be an **explanation of the effectiveness** of the contribution of literary/linguistic techniques to the impact of the text(s).	**Analysis** • There will be **some insight** shown into the **effectiveness** of the contribution of literary/linguistic techniques to the impact of the text(s).
	Evaluation • There will be **some engagement** with the text(s) which will state or imply an evaluation of its effectiveness.	**Evaluation** • There will be **engagement** with the text(s) which leads to a **generally valid** evaluative stance with respect to the text(s).	**Evaluation** • There will be a **clear engagement** with the text(s) which leads to a **valid** evaluative stance with respect to the material.
	Expression • Language will communicate the argument clearly, and there will be appropriate critical terminology deployed. Spelling, grammar and punctuation will be sufficiently accurate.	**Expression** • Language will communicate the argument **clearly**, and there will be appropriate critical terminology deployed to **aid the argument**. Spelling, grammar and punctuation will be sufficiently accurate.	**Expression** • The language will communicate **effectively** making appropriate use of critical terminology to **further the argument**. Spelling, grammar and punctuation will be sufficiently accurate.